CHRISTIAN COMMUNITY

ROB
SUGGS

10 STUDIES
FOR INDIVIDUALS
OR GROUPS

Builder
Study

INTER-VARSITY PRESS
36 Causton Street, London SW1P 4ST, England
Email: ivp@ivpbooks.com
Website: www.ivpbooks.com

Originally published in the United States of America in the LifeGuide® Bible Studies series in 2003 by InterVarsity Press, Downers Grove, Illinois
First published in Great Britain by Scripture Union in 2003
This edition published in Great Britain by Inter-Varsity Press 2018

British Library Cataloguing-in-Publication Data
A catalogue record for this book is available from the British Library.

ISBN: 978–1–78359–831–1

Printed in Great Britain by Ashford Colour Press Ltd, Gosport, Hampshire

Inter-Varsity Press publishes Christian books that are true to the Bible and that communicate the gospel, develop discipleship and strengthen the church for its mission in the world.

IVP originated within the Inter-Varsity Fellowship, now the Universities and Colleges Christian Fellowship, a student movement connecting Christian Unions in universities and colleges throughout Great Britain, and a member movement of the International Fellowship of Evangelical Students. Website: www.uccf.org.uk. That historic association is maintained, and all senior IVP staff and committee members subscribe to the UCCF Basis of Faith.

Contents

Getting the Most Out of *Christian Community*

The world is growing—and shrinking. Even as the global village adds thousands more each day, technology diminishes the gap between us. Through a video screen, a breaking news event can be shared in real time across the world. Rapid travel offers us unprecedented access to each other. We can communicate with others through a computer modem, a cellular car phone or a specialized support group. But all the while, surveys tell us that people believe loneliness to be their greatest problem.

We all yearn for a sense of community. As our world continues to urbanize, we have more acquaintances and fewer friends. The small-town neighborhood and parish church have given way to the high-rise condominium and megachurch. Our social calendars are filled, and we have an infinite variety of options in choosing how to spend time. But somehow at the end of the day we wonder if anyone really *knows* us.

The Bible describes a revolutionary community designed for any society, in any age. It offers the blueprint for a spiritual kingdom where the King's subjects are loved, nurtured and protected. In this kingdom, everyone has distinct gifts, yet differences bring people together. Anyone can be included, and no one is expendable. When the kingdom citizens are wounded, the community cares for them and restores their health. There is unconditional love, but uncompromising accountability. It's a center of never-ending joy, celebration and worship.

The Bible's most pervasive image for this new community is *family*. Amazingly, the Creator of the universe chooses to approach us as Father and invites us to enter into relationship with him as his children. And as the Father adopts us into his household, he introduces us to a wonderful extended family of brothers and sisters. The members of this family, like little children, make mistakes from time to time. They have quarrels, dishonor the family and disappoint their Father. Yet at other times they perform miracles. Ultimately, they constitute the most wonderful family we can ever claim. This is Christian community.

While you might certainly undertake this Bible study individually, *Christian Community* will have much to offer to groups. As you explore what it means to partake in the unique fellowship of the body of Christ, that fellowship can be enhanced in your group. In study eight on confession, for example, you might choose to have a cleansing time of confession in your group. The studies on worship and service would provide similar opportunities. This revision of the guide, prepared by Dale and Sandy Larsen, provides new features to enhance group life as you study together.

My prayer is that this guide will inspire, revitalize and empower the Christian relationships in your life so that you might one day have the experience of the early believers in Acts 2: the whole world will want the remarkable thing your community shares. For on our planet, every individual carries a deep desire to be "no longer foreigners and aliens, but fellow citizens with God's people and members of God's household" (Ephesians 2:19). May the study of God's Word be your guide down that road.

Suggestions for Individual Study

1. As you begin each study, pray that God will speak to you through his Word.

2. Read the introduction to the study and respond to the personal reflection question or exercise. This is designed to help you focus on God and on the theme of the study.

3. Each study deals with a particular passage—so that you can delve into the author's meaning in that context. Read and reread the passage to be studied. The questions are written using the language of the New International Version, so you may wish to use that version of the Bible. The New Revised Standard Version is also recommended.

4. This is an inductive Bible study, designed to help you discover for yourself what Scripture is saying. The study includes three types of questions. *Observation* questions ask about the basic facts: who, what, when, where and how. *Interpretation* questions delve into the meaning of the passage. *Application* questions help you discover the implications of the text for growing in Christ. These three keys unlock the treasures of Scripture.

Write your answers to the questions in the spaces provided or in a personal journal. Writing can bring clarity and deeper understanding of yourself and of God's Word.

5. It might be good to have a Bible dictionary handy. Use it to look up any unfamiliar words, names or places.

6. Use the prayer suggestion to guide you in thanking God for what you have learned and to pray about the applications that have come to mind.

7. You may want to go on to the suggestion under "Now or Later," or you may want to use that idea for your next study.

Suggestions for Members of a Group Study

1. Come to the study prepared. Follow the suggestions for individual study mentioned above. You will find that careful preparation will greatly enrich your time spent in group discussion.

2. Be willing to participate in the discussion. The leader of your group will not be lecturing. Instead, he or she will be encouraging the members of the group to discuss what they have learned. The leader will be asking the questions that are found in this guide.

3. Stick to the topic being discussed. Your answers should be based on the verses which are the focus of the discussion and not on outside authorities such as commentaries or speakers. These studies focus on a particular passage of Scripture. Only rarely should you refer to other portions of the Bible. This allows for everyone to participate in in-depth study on equal ground.

4. Be sensitive to the other members of the group. Listen attentively when they describe what they have learned. You may be surprised by their insights! Each question assumes a variety of answers. Many questions do not have "right" answers, particularly questions that aim at meaning or application. Instead the questions push us to explore the passage more thoroughly.

When possible, link what you say to the comments of others. Also, be affirming whenever you can. This will encourage some of the more hesitant members of the group to participate.

5. Be careful not to dominate the discussion. We are sometimes so eager to express our thoughts that we leave too little opportunity for others to respond. By all means participate! But allow others to also.

6. Expect God to teach you through the passage being discussed and through the other members of the group. Pray that you will have an enjoyable and profitable time together, but also that as a result of the study you will find ways that you can take action individually and/or as a group.

7. Remember that anything said in the group is considered confidential and should not be discussed outside the group unless specific permission is given to do so.

8. If you are the group leader, you will find additional suggestions at the back of the guide.

1

Built to Last

Ephesians 2:11-22

We fell in love with the house. Better yet, we fell in love with the price. This home had everything. How could it be such a financial bargain? Suddenly, we found out. As we walked down a hallway, there was a sensation of moving downhill. The building had a shifting foundation.

Much of life is as unstable as that house. "Secure" jobs evaporate in corporate downsizing. Friends move away or their values change, and they drift away from us. Even some churches divide over petty issues. How can we establish relationships that are built on a truly reliable foundation?

GROUP DISCUSSION. Have you ever belonged to an organization which, in your judgment, failed to be what you had envisioned? Discuss what elements may have contributed to its ineffectiveness.

PERSONAL REFLECTION. Think about negative experiences you've had with an organization or group. How did the experience affect your future involvement with organizations or groups?

The Christian community, according to the apostle Paul, has been built for us with strong and lasting materials. As you read, keep in mind that the first Christians were Jewish. As non-Jews (Gentiles) began to join the faith, they did not share the religious and cultural heritage of the Jewish people. The church decided very early that the

Jewish rite of circumcision was not necessary for a Gentile who accepted Christ (Acts 15:1-21). *Read Ephesians 2:11-22.*

---

1. How would you describe Paul's emotions about Christ and the church?

---

2. What was the relationship between Jew and Gentile before Christ came (vv. 11-13)?

---

3. What differences in background and culture threaten the unity of your own church?

---

4. Explain what Paul means by the "dividing wall of hostility" (v. 14).

---

5. Christ himself "is our peace" (v. 14). How did he accomplish this peace (vv. 14-18)?

6. How do “dividing walls of hostility” keep people from hearing the gospel today?

---

7. What barriers stood in the way of your putting faith in Christ, and how did God overcome them?

---

8. In verse 19 Paul compares Christians to citizens and family members. In what ways does each of these two comparisons hold true?

---

9. In your own church, who are some people you would describe as “good citizens” or “good family members” (v. 19)?

---

10. What building materials make up the construction described in verses 20-22?

11. The apostles and prophets (v. 20) can represent the New Testament and Old Testament. Why are the Scriptures vital as the foundation of our Christian community?

---

12. Verse 22 identifies the true resident of the "building." How does his presence affect your attitude toward the church?

---

13. In your relationship to your own church, consider ways in which you might resemble a pile of stones lying off to one side, instead of an integral part of the building. How will you become a more functional part of this dwelling place of God that is under construction (v. 21)?

Pray that your church will grow into the kind of spiritual temple that Paul evokes. Pray especially that your own involvement in the church will further that growth.

Now or Later

This week try to be aware of what sort of "brick" or "stone" you are in the spiritual dwelling which is the church. Ask yourself, *Am I too much of an individual, not fitting into the whole? Do I take on too great a role as though I want to control the entire building? Do I appreciate the value of the other parts of the building?*

2

Everyone's Involved

1 Corinthians 12

Melba is totally dedicated to developing her gift of playing the oboe. An orchestra is too restrictive for her progress in "oboism" because she has to yield to too many other instruments. So she has sought out other oboists and created an all-oboe orchestra. Not surprisingly, tickets for the first concert have moved very slowly.

GROUP DISCUSSION. What abilities do you appreciate about each other? Take a few minutes to name some things. You might praise talents such as musical or athletic ability, but also try to concentrate on character qualities such as encouragement, hospitality or compassion.

PERSONAL REFLECTION. What unique ability or talent do you most enjoy using?

The church in Corinth was a collection of "soloists" who needed to learn to play in harmony. They had a nightmarish list of problems, including bitter strife, sexual immorality and drunkenness at the Lord's Supper! Paul sets forth the picture of a church where everyone has a part and all parts fit together into a whole. *Read 1 Corinthians 12:1-11.*

---

1. What is Paul's central message for the Christians in Corinth?

---

2. When have you needed the same sort of advice Paul gave the Corinthians?

---

3. Contrast the Corinthians' previous lives as pagans and their present lives as Christian believers (vv. 1-3).

---

4. Given the common source of all spiritual gifts, what should be their results (vv. 4-7)?

What factors might cause the outcome to be otherwise?

5. How do each of the gifts mentioned in verses 8-10 contribute to the unity of the church?

---

6. *Read 1 Corinthians 12:12-31.* In what ways is the human body an appropriate metaphor for the church of Jesus Christ?

---

7. How should each of us be personally encouraged by the truth about gifts in verse 18?

---

8. According to Paul, how can we avoid divisions in the church (vv. 21-25)?

---

9. Look again at verses 21-25. In what ways have you failed to give honor to the weaker parts of the body of Christ?

10. What are some practical ways to give honor to those "parts of the body" which are typically regarded as "less honorable" (v. 23)?

---

11. Focus on verses 27-31. What do you consider to be your spiritual gift(s)?

---

12. How will you seek "the greater gifts" (v. 31)?

Ask for the Lord's forgiveness for any selfish ways you have used your gifts. If you are studying in a group, express prayers of thankfulness for one another's gifts.

Now or Later

How are you currently using your spiritual gifts to strengthen community in your church?

This week, how will you seek to use your gifts to serve others?

3

Everyone's Invited

Philemon

My friend Ray was a dealer in illegal drugs, but meeting Christ brought radical change to his life. He is now one of our church's most enthusiastic members. Well-dressed and socially adept, Ray found quick acceptance and blended easily.

One day Ray brought with him two friends struggling with substance abuse. Their hair was unkempt, they wore "street clothing," and they were wary of unfamiliar church surroundings. As Ray introduced them to an elderly woman during the service, the woman coldly turned away without speaking. Their suspicions confirmed, the pair hasn't returned.

GROUP DISCUSSION. Compose an invitation which you would like very much to receive:

____

invites you to

____

on

____

at

____

PERSONAL REFLECTION. Think of a time you failed to get an invitation when it seemed everyone else was invited. How did you feel?

The fellowship of believers is intended to be a place of healing, forgiveness and equality. In a short letter, Paul urges Philemon and his church to restore to their membership a runaway slave, Onesimus. *Read Philemon.*

---

1. What does Paul hope to accomplish by writing this letter?

---

2. Paul's other writings show he could express himself in a very authoritative manner. How would you describe the tone of this letter?

---

3. Think of a time you were asked (or expected) to include someone who was undesirable. How did you respond?

---

4. How does Paul encourage his readers (vv. 1-7)?

---

5. What appeal does he then make to them (vv. 8-11)?

6. Onesimus's name means "useful." How does Paul play on this name in verse 11?

Why do you think Paul made this pun in a serious letter?

---

7. What changes are implied in Onesimus's life (vv. 10-12)?

---

8. Despite the changes, why was Onesimus an unlikely candidate for full acceptance into the church?

---

9. How does Paul build a case for reconciliation in verses 12-22?

---

10. What types of people are unlikely candidates for acceptance in your church?

11. Martin Luther wrote, "Even as Christ did for us with God the Father, thus Paul also does for Onesimus with Philemon." How does Paul use his own standing with his readers to further the cause of Onesimus? (See especially vv. 17-18.)

---

12. How can you stand up for those whom your church might overlook or even reject?

Pray for those who need to feel included in your group or church. Avoid general prayers and consider specific names of people.

Now or Later

Make plans to get to know someone in your church whom you have overlooked. Also make plans to reach out to someone who is not yet part of your church but who needs to find welcome there.

4

We Gather Together

Psalm 100

You've heard the line. A seeker is invited to church but politely declines: "I can worship just as well while working in my garden or away at the lake. I don't need to be sitting in some expensive church sanctuary."

It's a common notion: worship, even religious faith itself, is a personal and private matter. Certainly worship must come from one's own heart, and anyone can praise God in solitude. But the Bible teaches that God is pleased by worship that occurs together, in community. Any family has a traditional, meaningful place to gather, such as at the dinner table or around the Christmas tree. God's family is no different.

GROUP DISCUSSION. Describe a worship service that was particularly meaningful to you. Try to get beyond features of "worship style" and talk about why that time touched you especially deeply.

PERSONAL REFLECTION. What are the most important aspects of worship for you?

Some of the psalms are personal; others express and encourage group worship. While Psalm 23 is the most cherished personal psalm, Psalm 100 is the best-loved "community" psalm. *Read Psalm 100.*

---

1. What evidence do you find that this psalm encourages group worship rather than individual worship?

---

2. Who or what encourages you to gather with other believers in worship?

---

3. Where is the focus of this psalm?

---

4. In this psalm, what are worshipers urged to do? (Look for specific commands or instructions.)

---

5. The "gates" and the "courts" of verse 4 refer to the temple of the Lord in Jerusalem. Why is it important to have a special place of worship?

6. For what reasons are we to "enter his gates with thanksgiving and his courts with praise" (vv. 4-5)?

---

7. Why are thanks and praise essential elements of worship?

---

8. How can corporate worship help our personal worship when we don't feel particularly thankful or full of praise?

---

9. Why do you think some Christians avoid corporate worship?

---

10. The psalms are actually songs, although the tunes are lost to us. How do the songs you sing tell of God's love and faithfulness?

---

11. What story of God's love and faithfulness can you share, perhaps from your own family history?

12. What opportunities do you have this week to join in corporate worship?

---

13. How will you take advantage of those opportunities?

Pray that your experiences of community worship will be marked with joy and dedication to Christ. Ask the Lord to protect your church from strife that distracts from and interferes with worship.

Now or Later

Taking off from question 11, write a psalm which tells a story of the Lord's goodness in your life, the life of your family, your church or someone else you know. Plan a time to get together and read your psalms to one another. Make this a time of mutual encouragement and corporate praise.

5

Community Commissioned

Luke 10:1-20

The word *evangelism* summons many colorful images. Some think immediately of the street-corner character, preaching and pounding his Bible as folks quickly walk by. Some picture the television preachers who inhabit certain cable channels. Others think about a big arena crusade, with the converted pouring down the aisles as the "invitation" music plays. For many of us, the word *evangelism* inspires feelings of vague uneasiness and guilt.

GROUP DISCUSSION. Which of these words or phrases come to your mind when you think of the word *evangelism?*

☐ pressure
☐ sharing the good news
☐ TV preachers
☐ guilt that I don't do it enough
☐ a crusade in a big arena with a famous preacher
☐ going out on the streets talking to strangers
☐ fear
☐ a church committee
☐ other:_______________

PERSONAL REFLECTION. What are some reasons you may hesitate to share your faith with someone?

Few associate evangelism with community activity. In the New Testament, however, it is almost always a pair or group of believers who share their faith. Even Paul traveled with partners. Luke's Gospel gives an account of Jesus commissioning his community to spread their faith (Luke 9:1-6). Later he sent out a larger group of followers on a similar mission. *Read Luke 10:1-20.*

---

1. What are some appealing and unappealing features of the work Jesus gave these seventy-two people?

---

2. When has the Lord given you a job that had both blessings and dangers?

---

3. Why do you think Jesus sent these people out in pairs (v. 1)?

---

4. How do you account for Jesus' two prohibitions in verse 4?

5. How do those cautions apply to believers today who want to carry out Jesus' mission?

---

6. Consider the responsibility given to believers in verse 16. How should that encourage us?

---

7. How should that responsibility humble us?

---

8. What was the response of the seventy-two to their completed mission (v. 17)?

---

9. How did Jesus characterize the nature of their mission (vv. 18-19)?

---

10. Jesus cautioned against an attitude of spiritual arrogance in verse 20. How might a Christian who is active in witnessing fall into such arrogance?

11. What are some ways your community of believers reaches out to others in active witness?

---

12. How can your community of believers work together to better carry out the work of evangelism?

---

13. What role do you see yourself playing in the evangelistic work of your fellowship?

Pray for people who need to come to faith in Christ. Pray also for each other, that you will encourage each other in the work of evangelism. Ask the Lord to give your fellowship opportunities to witness and the courage and wisdom to follow through.

Now or Later

Brainstorm ways your group can plan an outreach activity. It can be anything that brings you into positive and friendly contact with people who need your witness.

6

Servant's Entrance

Matthew 25:31-46

Church life is full of opportunities to serve. Scan the Sunday bulletin or listen to the announcements, and you'll hear many appeals for help. It seems there are always more jobs than people willing to do them. Soon opportunity begins to look like obligation. How often has someone approached you with a look of desperation and said, "You're the perfect person for this job, and besides, nobody else will do it"?

By contrast, we usually jump at opportunities to get together and have fun. We're quick to sign up for a church picnic or camping trip or movie night. Ironically, nothing builds true community like selfless service together. Many Christian groups form strong bonds of fellowship as they give of their time and sweat in ministry together.

GROUP DISCUSSION. What is the most meaningful act of service that a group has ever provided to you or your family?

PERSONAL REFLECTION. Which have you found more rewarding—being served or serving? Why?

In the last week of Jesus' earthly life he came to Jerusalem, the center of Jewish spiritual and political life and the site of God's temple. Sitting on the Mount of Olives opposite the temple, he talked about his future return and how Christians should behave in the interim. Then he painted a vivid word picture of future judgment. *Read Matthew 25:31-46.*

---

1. What contrasts are made throughout this passage?

---

2. In Jesus' story, what is the setting (v. 31)?

---

3. On what basis are the "sheep and goats" divided (vv. 34-36)?

---

4. What thoughts and feelings do you have as you think about the division of the sheep and the goats?

---

5. As you imagine yourself before the throne on that day, with which group do you see yourself being put, and why?

---

6. What do the services described in verses 35-36 have in common?

---

7. Why do you think those on the king's right are surprised by what he says (vv. 37-39)?

8. It is possible to read this story and conclude that we must earn salvation through our actions. How do you respond to that interpretation, and why?

---

9. In what sense is Jesus hungry, thirsty, a stranger, in need of clothing, sick and in prison (vv. 40, 45)?

---

10. What, for you, would be the effect of seeing Jesus himself in the faces of helpless people?

---

11. What does this passage say to you about the priority of service in your own Christian community?

---

12. What practical changes can you and your church bring about to make service a higher priority?

Pray for God to create in you the heart of a servant. Pray for faithful servants of God in your church and community.

Now or Later

Come up with more answers to question 12, and consider how to put one or more of them into practice. Identify resources you will need and people to invite on board. As you plan, keep in mind the need to develop a servant's heart rather than to work for any selfish motives or to earn salvation.

7

And They'll Know We Are Christians

John 13:1-17, 34-35

I ❤ NY. I ❤ skiing. I ❤ my dachshund. Our society is obsessed with the concept of love. We've enshrined it and romanticized it. At the same time, we have trivialized it and reduced it to a bumper sticker symbol. The Bible's definition of *love* is radically different from our culture's prevailing idea of love. The biblical idea liberates us from the shifting whims of popular opinion.

GROUP DISCUSSION. Name some recent movies and popular songs on the theme of love. What message did they carry about the subject?

PERSONAL REFLECTION. Write two definitions of *love:* one from a worldly perspective and one from a Christian perspective.

The scene is the Last Supper. Jesus is about to die and knows it. He has tried to tell his disciples, but they don't want to hear it. At the time when they should be most united, they revive an old argument about which of them is the greatest (Luke 22:24). Jesus takes action to teach them about love. *Read John 13:1-17, 34-35.*

1. What filled Jesus' thoughts as this scene began (vv. 1-3)?

---

2. Picture yourself as one of the disciples. Describe Jesus' actions in verses 4-6 from your perspective.

---

3. How would you have reacted when you saw Jesus do the things in verses 4 and 5?

---

4. Why did Peter object so strongly (vv. 6-8)?

---

5. What had Peter realized to make him respond as he did in verse 9?

---

6. Imagine that you are the next disciple after Peter. What do you say and do when Jesus kneels before you to wash your feet?

---

7. How did Jesus intend for the disciples to take his example and put it into action (vv. 12-17)?

8. What should be a Christian's standard for loving (v. 34)?

---

9. How will love affect the disciples' standing in the world (v. 35)?

---

10. What does this say about the world's own version of love?

---

11. What "foot washing" have members of your church performed for one another recently?

---

12. How can you do some "foot washing" for someone in your fellowship this week?

Pray that God will build your fellowship's mutual love, to the point that outsiders will recognize without doubt that you are Jesus' followers.

Now or Later

None of the disciples expected their Teacher and Lord to do such a humble act of service as washing their feet. What is an act of service that you consider beneath you? Imagine Jesus doing that action, and then follow his example.

8

True Confessions

Nehemiah 9:1-5; James 5:13-20

The classic play and movie *Twelve Angry Men* deals with the jury in a murder trial. In the beginning, the twelve know nothing about each other. They are simply juror number one, juror number two and so on. They discuss the case with detachment. But as the hours wear on and the tension builds, the reserve of each begins to melt away. The jurors begin to share facts about themselves—facts that often reveal their biases. The seclusion of the jury room brings down barriers, encourages honesty and builds a community. The Christian community also involves transparency, and it may take stress to bring it about.

GROUP DISCUSSION. What group of people during the last few years have you been the most open and transparent with? Why?

PERSONAL REFLECTION. Do you find it helpful to tell your sins to another person? Why or why not?

The book of Nehemiah tells of the rebuilding of Jerusalem's walls—and its community—after a generation of foreign exile and captivity in Babylon. When the walls were completed, Ezra the priest began to read the book of the Law to the assembled people. After celebrating the Feast of Tabernacles for seven days, the people regathered to confess their sins. *Read Nehemiah 9:1-5.*

---

1. What was the mood of this assembly?

---

2. How did the Israelites prepare for confession (vv. 1-2)?

---

3. Does the idea of public confession of sin appeal to you or repel you? Explain why you respond as you do.

---

4. How did the Israelites use their time at the confessional gathering (vv. 2-3)?

---

5. The reading of the Law (the first five books of the Old Testament) was followed by confession and worship (v. 3). Why do both make sense as a response to hearing God's Word?

---

6. Levites (vv. 4-5) were the priests of Israel. How can church leaders be involved in helping the Christian community in confession?

---

7. Nehemiah 9 portrays people confessing sin with each other. Many years later, James wrote about confessing sin to each other—a more difficult and humbling challenge. *Read James 5:13-20.* What point does James make about trouble, happiness and illness in verses 13 and 14?

8. How are confession and corporate prayer connected (vv. 14-16)?

---

9. What example of righteous praying does James set forth in verses 17-18?

---

10. How does James stress the urgency of our accountability to each other (vv. 19-20)?

---

11. What are some helpful guidelines you've learned for when, how and what to confess to others?

---

12. In what areas do you need to become more transparent with your fellow believers?

Pray for courage to confess your sins honestly and promptly before God. Pray for more honesty with others concerning your struggles with sin. At the same time, pray for wisdom that confession will never be inappropriate or self-serving.

Now or Later

If you are studying in a group, have a time of repentance when each person writes specific sins privately on paper. Some may be read aloud if appropriate. Pray for each other in your struggles with sin. Read aloud several Scriptures about the mercy of God in Christ. Then burn the papers together. Sing some songs of thankfulness for Jesus' death on the cross for you.

9

Confrontation & Restoration

Matthew 18:15-35

There's the tale of the father who had fallen out with his son. After a time, he posted this sign in the town square: Son—all is forgiven. Meet me here at sunset. At the appointed time, seventy-five young men showed up.

How many broken relationships among our friends and families are never repaired? Why are church splits so common? Perhaps many of us don't know how to lovingly handle conflict, reconciliation and forgiveness.

GROUP DISCUSSION. How do you feel after an argument with a friend?

☐ terrible ☐ angry ☐ embarrassed
☐ justified ☐ regretful ☐ relieved
☐ other:____________________

PERSONAL REFLECTION. How do you tend to handle conflict?

Even when Jesus' followers were still few, they already had questions about how to get along with each other. *Read Matthew 18:15-20.*

---

1. In general, what sort of situation among Christians is Jesus talking about?

2. Without giving unnecessary detail, how have you experienced this type of situation in the church?

---

3. What wisdom is there in confronting an offender alone (v. 15)?

---

4. What might be added by involving one or two other people (v. 16)?

---

5. To what additional levels of confrontation should we proceed, and why (v. 17)?

---

6. In the quiet of your own heart, consider a time when you have confronted someone about a wrong. How did your experience compare with verses 15-17?

---

7. How do verses 18-20 affirm the reconciling power of praying together?

---

8. In response to Jesus' teaching about how to approach someone who has done wrong, Peter asked a question. The query motivated Jesus to tell a parable. *Read Matthew 18:21-35.* What is the progression of events in the story?

9. Ten thousand talents (v. 24) would equal millions of dollars, a sum no one could have paid. Why do you think Jesus used such a staggering total in his story?

---

10. How would it be possible for the forgiven man to so quickly turn on his fellow servant without mercy?

---

11. In what ways are you like the angry servant in verse 28?

---

12. How can your church or fellowship group apply the wisdom of this passage to the conflicts you face?

---

13. What step(s) will you take to put this passage into action?

Think about people you need to forgive. Pray for them. Ask God to help you show them the same mercy which Christ has shown to you.

Now or Later

Put on a dramatization of Jesus' parable in Matthew 18:23-34. The story has potential for humor, without neglecting its serious meaning.

10

A Haven for Healing

Ezekiel 34:1-16

I recently heard of a Sunday school class whose members really love each other. When one of them experienced a stroke and paralysis, she became homebound. She grieved for the fellowship of the class, and they missed her as well. So the members pooled their funds and purchased a video camera. Each week, they film the class lesson and discussion, making special comments and greetings to their absent friend. For her, it's almost as good as being there.

GROUP DISCUSSION. The last time you were ill for an extended period of time, how were you cared for and by whom?

PERSONAL REFLECTION. How do you feel when you have to depend on others?

In the King's community, the citizens are protected, loved and healed. The prophet Ezekiel offers a prophetic warning against forsaking that task. *Read Ezekiel 34:1-16.*

---

1. Describe the situation in Israel according to these verses.

2. According to verses 4-5, what were five responsibilities which Israel's leaders had failed to carry out?

---

3. What were the tragic results of the leaders' failure to carry out their mission (vv. 1-8)?

---

4. Consider a church or fellowship where the leaders do carry out faithfully the responsibilities of verses 4-5. What difference does their faithfulness make in the life of that group?

---

5. How did the Lord react to the unfaithful shepherds' behavior (vv. 7-10)?

---

6. Count the number of times the word *I* occurs in verses 11-16 (God speaking). What does the repetition of that little word tell you about God?

---

7. What else do we learn about the Lord's character from his words in verses 11-16?

---

8. Although the Lord himself steps in to fill the leadership gap, it is clear from verses 1-8 that he desires his appointed leaders to do their jobs. What are your own God-given responsibilities in the church?

---

9. Where are you tempted to slack off in your responsibilities to God's "flock"?

---

10. How can you encourage the leaders of your fellowship to take more seriously their responsibilities to the weak, as suggested by this passage?

---

11. This week, what is one way you will personally address one or more of the responsibilities of verse 5?

- ☐ strengthen the weak
- ☐ bring back the strays
- ☐ heal the sick
- ☐ search for the lost
- ☐ bind up the injured

---

12. What will you do to help your church carry out each of those tasks?

Ask God to show you the weak, wounded and lost you've been called to heal, and to move you to positive action.

Now or Later

Draw a picture or write a description of what your church would look like if it were truly a "haven for healing." Keep it where you will see it frequently, so it reminds you to both pray and work toward making that vision reality. Feel free to revise the picture or written description as you get more insight into what makes a church that sort of healing fellowship.

Leader's Notes

MY GRACE IS SUFFICIENT FOR YOU. (2 COR 12:9)

Leading a Bible discussion can be an enjoyable and rewarding experience. But it can also be *scary*—especially if you've never done it before. If this is your feeling, you're in good company. When God asked Moses to lead the Israelites out of Egypt, he replied, "O Lord, please send someone else to do it"! (Ex 4:13). It was the same with Solomon, Jeremiah and Timothy, but God helped these people in spite of their weaknesses, and he will help you as well.

You don't need to be an expert on the Bible or a trained teacher to lead a Bible discussion. The idea behind these inductive studies is that the leader guides group members to discover for themselves what the Bible has to say. This method of learning will allow group members to remember much more of what is said than a lecture would.

These studies are designed to be led easily. As a matter of fact, the flow of questions through the passage from observation to interpretation to application is so natural that you may feel that the studies lead themselves. This study guide is also flexible. You can use it with a variety of groups—student, professional, neighborhood or church groups. Each study takes forty-five to sixty minutes in a group setting.

There are some important facts to know about group dynamics and encouraging discussion. The suggestions listed below should enable you to effectively and enjoyably fulfill your role as leader.

Preparing for the Study

1. Ask God to help you understand and apply the passage in your own life. Unless this happens, you will not be prepared to lead others. Pray too for the various members of the group. Ask God to open your hearts to the message of his Word and motivate you to action.

2. Read the introduction to the entire guide to get an overview of the

entire book and the issues which will be explored.

3. As you begin each study, read and reread the assigned Bible passage to familiarize yourself with it.

4. This study guide is based on the New International Version of the Bible. It will help you and the group if you use this translation as the basis for your study and discussion.

5. Carefully work through each question in the study. Spend time in meditation and reflection as you consider how to respond.

6. Write your thoughts and responses in the space provided in the study guide. This will help you to express your understanding of the passage clearly.

7. It might help to have a Bible dictionary handy. Use it to look up any unfamiliar words, names or places. (For additional help on how to study a passage, see chapter five of *How to Lead a LifeBuilder Study*, IVP, 2018.)

8. Consider how you can apply the Scripture to your life. Remember that the group will follow your lead in responding to the studies. They will not go any deeper than you do.

9. Once you have finished your own study of the passage, familiarize yourself with the leader's notes for the study you are leading. These are designed to help you in several ways. First, they tell you the purpose the study guide author had in mind when writing the study. Take time to think through how the study questions work together to accomplish that purpose. Second, the notes provide you with additional background information or suggestions on group dynamics for various questions. This information can be useful when people have difficulty understanding or answering a question. Third, the leader's notes can alert you to potential problems you may encounter during the study.

10. If you wish to remind yourself of anything mentioned in the leader's notes, make a note to yourself below that question in the study.

Leading the Study

1. Begin the study on time. Open with prayer, asking God to help the group to understand and apply the passage.

2. Be sure that everyone in your group has a study guide. Encourage the group to prepare beforehand for each discussion by reading the introduction to the guide and by working through the questions in the study.

3. At the beginning of your first time together, explain that these studies are meant to be discussions, not lectures. Encourage the members of the group to participate. However, do not put pressure on those who may be hesitant

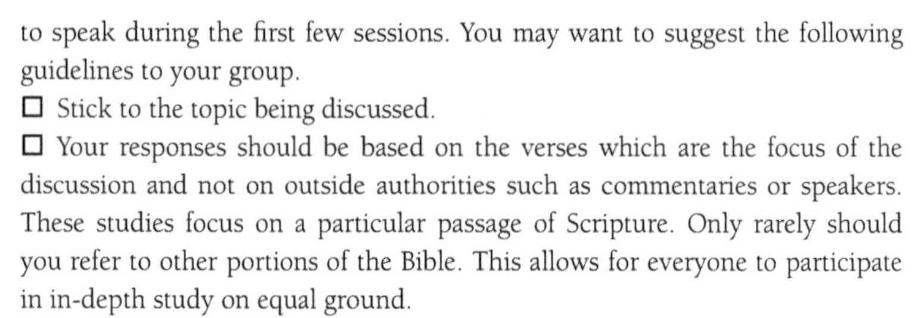

to speak during the first few sessions. You may want to suggest the following guidelines to your group.

☐ Stick to the topic being discussed.

☐ Your responses should be based on the verses which are the focus of the discussion and not on outside authorities such as commentaries or speakers. These studies focus on a particular passage of Scripture. Only rarely should you refer to other portions of the Bible. This allows for everyone to participate in in-depth study on equal ground.

☐ Anything said in the group is considered confidential and will not be discussed outside the group unless specific permission is given to do so.

☐ We will listen attentively to each other and provide time for each person present to talk.

☐ We will pray for each other.

4. Have a group member read the introduction at the beginning of the discussion.

5. Every session begins with a group discussion question. The question or activity is meant to be used before the passage is read. The question introduces the theme of the study and encourages group members to begin to open up. Encourage as many members as possible to participate, and be ready to get the discussion going with your own response.

This section is designed to reveal where our thoughts or feelings need to be transformed by Scripture. That is why it is especially important not to read the passage before the discussion question is asked. The passage will tend to color the honest reactions people would otherwise give because they are, of course, supposed to think the way the Bible does.

You may want to supplement the group discussion question with an icebreaker to help people to get comfortable. See the community section of the *Small Group Starter Kit* (IVP, 1995) for more ideas.

You also might want to use the personal reflection question with your group. Either allow a time of silence for people to respond individually or discuss it together.

6. Have a group member (or members if the passage is long) read aloud the passage to be studied. Then give people several minutes to read the passage again silently so that they can take it all in.

7. Question 1 will generally be an overview question designed to briefly survey the passage. Encourage the group to look at the whole passage, but try to avoid getting sidetracked by questions or issues that will be addressed later in the study.

8. As you ask the questions, keep in mind that they are designed to be used just as they are written. You may simply read them aloud. Or you may prefer to express them in your own words.

There may be times when it is appropriate to deviate from the study guide. For example, a question may have already been answered. If so, move on to the next question. Or someone may raise an important question not covered in the guide. Take time to discuss it, but try to keep the group from going off on tangents.

9. Avoid answering your own questions. If necessary, repeat or rephrase them until they are clearly understood. Or point out something you read in the leader's notes to clarify the context or meaning. An eager group quickly becomes passive and silent if they think the leader will do most of the talking.

10. Don't be afraid of silence. People may need time to think about the question before formulating their answers.

11. Don't be content with just one answer. Ask, "What do the rest of you think?" or "Anything else?" until several people have given answers to the question.

12. Acknowledge all contributions. Try to be affirming whenever possible. Never reject an answer. If it is clearly off-base, ask, "Which verse led you to that conclusion?" or again, "What do the rest of you think?"

13. Don't expect every answer to be addressed to you, even though this will probably happen at first. As group members become more at ease, they will begin to truly interact with each other. This is one sign of healthy discussion.

14. Don't be afraid of controversy. It can be very stimulating. If you don't resolve an issue completely, don't be frustrated. Move on and keep it in mind for later. A subsequent study may solve the problem.

15. Periodically summarize what the group has said about the passage. This helps to draw together the various ideas mentioned and gives continuity to the study. But don't preach.

16. At the end of the Bible discussion you may want to allow group members a time of quiet to work on an idea under "Now or Later." Then discuss what you experienced. Or you may want to encourage group members to work on these ideas between meetings. Give an opportunity during the session for people to talk about what they are learning.

17. Conclude your time together with conversational prayer, adapting the prayer suggestion at the end of the study to your group. Ask for God's help in following through on the commitments you've made.

18. End on time.

Many more suggestions and helps are found in *How to Lead a LifeBuilder Study*.

Components of Small Groups

A healthy small group should do more than study the Bible. There are four components to consider as you structure your time together.

Nurture. Small groups help us to grow in our knowledge and love of God. Bible study is the key to making this happen and is the foundation of your small group.

Community. Small groups are a great place to develop deep friendships with other Christians. Allow time for informal interaction before and after each study. Plan activities and games that will help you get to know each other. Spend time having fun together—going on a picnic or cooking dinner together.

Worship and prayer. Your study will be enhanced by spending time praising God together in prayer or song. Pray for each other's needs—and keep track of how God is answering prayer in your group. Ask God to help you to apply what you are learning in your study.

Outreach. Reaching out to others can be a practical way of applying what you are learning, and it will keep your group from becoming self-focused. Host a series of evangelistic discussions for your friends or neighbors. Clean up the yard of an elderly friend. Serve at a soup kitchen together, or spend a day working in the community.

Many more suggestions and helps in each of these areas are found in the *Small Group Starter Kit*. You will also find information on building a small group. Reading through the starter kit will be worth your time.

Study 1. Built to Last.
Ephesians 2:11-22.

Purpose: To discover the source, foundation and composition of the unique fellowship Christians find in community with each other.

General note. This is a crucial study intended to build a foundation for the rest of the study. Yet your group may not be accustomed to each other. As much as possible, try to be sure that before you begin the study, members have spent some time together, are comfortable with each other and are prepared to "hit the ground running" as they open God's Word.

Group discussion. Every study begins with a group discussion question, which is meant to be asked before the Scripture passage is read. These questions have several goals.

First, they help break the ice. No matter how well a group may know each other, there is some stiffness which needs to be overcome before people will begin to talk openly.

Second, they focus people's thinking on the topic of the study. Group members will be preoccupied with different things which have nothing to do with the study. A creative question gets their attention and draws them into the subject at hand.

Third, group discussion questions can reveal where our thoughts or feelings need to be transformed by Scripture. That is why it is important not to read the passage before the group discussion. Giving honest responses before they find out what the Bible says may help group members see where their thoughts or attitudes need to be changed.

In your group discussion for this study, steer the conversation away from churches and other Christian groups for now. We will examine those in later questions.

Personal reflection. These questions are written for those doing the studies on their own for personal growth. However, at times you may also want to use these questions in place of or in addition to the suggested group discussion.

Background note. While imprisoned in Rome, the apostle Paul wrote this letter we call Ephesians to Gentile Christians in Ephesus, on the west coast of modern Turkey. Paul had been arrested in Jerusalem for supposedly taking an Ephesian man (a Gentile) into the Jewish temple (Acts 21:27-29).

Question 2. Israel considered itself the special people of God. They had received God's revealed law and his particular blessings. With a few exceptions, Gentiles were considered outside the promises of God. Refer also to the introductory paragraph beginning "The first Christians were Jewish."

Question 3. Some group members may wish to answer this question privately. However, your group may be a safe place to bring up some chronic and potentially harmful misunderstandings. If your group members are all from one church, they may mention issues that surprise each other. If your group comes from various churches, it may be enlightening to hear about issues in different churches.

Question 4. The wall can be taken metaphorically, but it also had a literal meaning. Paul had been arrested on the charge of bringing a Gentile into the temple in Jerusalem (see the introductory paragraph). "Taking a non-Jew beyond a particular dividing point in the temple was such an important breach of Jewish law that the Romans even permitted Jewish leaders to execute violators of this law. Paul's readers in Ephesus and Asia undoubtedly know why Paul is in prison (Acts 21:27, 29); thus for them, as well as for Paul, there can be no greater symbol of the barrier between Jew and non-Jew than 'the dividing wall' of verse 14. But Paul says that this dividing wall is shattered in Christ" (Craig S. Keener, ed., *The IVP Bible Background Commentary: New Testament* [Downers Grove, Ill.: InterVarsity Press, 1993], p. 544).

Question 5. The cross is the key. Christ's sacrificial death made peace between God and humanity, and here Paul emphasizes that it also made peace among humanity. Be sure everyone understands just how Christ "destroyed the barrier." Sin in our lives alienates us from God and, therefore, from each other. Without dealing with the problem of our sin, there could ultimately be no fellowship with our Creator and Sustainer, and no community with our fellow humans. The cross destroyed that sin barrier forever.

Question 6. The "walls" can work two ways. Some walls keep potential believers from listening, such as preconceived negative ideas of Christianity or a home environment where faith is absent. Some walls inhibit Christians from witnessing, such as a sense of superiority to people of a certain social class. Even walls that divide a congregation can keep a church so preoccupied with its own problems it has no time or energy for outreach.

Question 7. Encourage group members to consider walls they once put up, as well as walls that were put up by others.

Question 8. Paul's metaphors, such as these two, help clarify his meanings. Also, they are always rich sources of application. Encourage your group to stretch to find as many parallels as possible, in this and in the next few questions.

Question 10. Christ as cornerstone, apostles and prophets as foundation, ourselves as stones or bricks. Since we are prone to think of the church as a building, this is a good place to remind the group that Paul refers not to a physical building but to the spiritual temple of Christians' lives. Be sure your group takes in the comprehensive and eloquent picture of the Christian community as a dwelling place which stands on the tangible, solid foundation of Scripture and is lived in and cared for by the loving presence of God's Spirit. We Christians are the bricks bound together by holy cement, supporting the eternal temple. This is a new way for most of us to see the church: it's a spiritual dwelling place on earth for the Spirit of God, just as the temple in Jerusalem once formed an earthly dwelling place.

Question 11. Your group's involvement in this Bible study shows that you emphasize Scripture study. Encourage members to share how the Bible has affected them and helped their faith. The Bible is the authority to which the Christian community turns for teaching and guidance. Without it, we would be at the mercy of various people's opinions.

Question 12. It is easy to sense God's presence in the natural world, but often it is much harder to sense God in other believers. If we keep in mind that God lives in us and in our fellow believers, we will honor them and wish them only the best; we will also treat ourselves with self-respect and refrain from doing anything to harm our bodies or our souls. Also, we will expect the Holy Spirit to energize us and give us wisdom and strength to do God's will.
Question 13. Answers may vary depending on whether all group members are from one church or are from diverse churches.

Study 2. Everyone's Involved. 1 Corinthians 12.
Purpose: To understand the place of spiritual gifts in building unity in the body of Christ.
Group Discussion. As the group leader, come equipped with a word of praise for each person so that no one goes without affirmation. Try to prevent the group from heaping compliments on one member and ignoring others. Even if your group members do not yet know each other well, this question can help them begin to express sincere appreciation for good qualities they have seen in one another so far. While you should steer the discussion toward character qualities rather than natural talents, be aware that a natural talent can be used by God as a spiritual gift.
Question 1. Paul's central message is that, although gifts may bring about conflict, their godly purpose is precisely the opposite: unity.
Question 4. Gifts from the Holy Spirit should promote "the common good" (v. 7). They should bring unity, for they come from the same God. When individual believers are proud, judgmental and selfish, the use of the Spirit's gifts leads to self-promotion, divisiveness and jealousy.
Questions 6-7. Paul presents a beautiful and rich biological metaphor for the church—and in truth it is more than metaphor. Whenever we come across such a word picture in Scripture, it pays to take time to explore the full range of the comparison. Philip Yancey and Dr. Paul Brand have written an entire book pursuing the intersection of the spiritual and the biological, *Fearfully and Wonderfully Made* (Zondervan, 1980). This image of the community as a spiritual body recurs at least thirty times in the New Testament. In his book *The Body* Charles Colson explains: "Ekklesia, the Greek word translated 'church' in the New Testament, never refers to a building or a structure. An ekklesia was a gathering of people. . . . But it is more than simply a collection of people; it is a new community. . . . When we confess Christ, God's response is to bring us into His church; we become part of His called-out people. When we become followers of Christ, we become members of His church—

and our commitment to the church is indistinguishable from our commitment to Him" (Charles Colson, with Ellen Santilli Vaughn, *The Body* [Dallas: Word, 1992], pp. 64-65).

Those who perform what are considered menial tasks in the church—making coffee or vacuuming the floor—have equal value with preachers, teachers and musicians. In a status-obsessed world, this is a difficult truth even for Christians to digest.

Question 8. A follow-up question would be, "What happens to a physical body when its parts do not work together properly?"

Question 10. Take this question out of the theoretical realm by mentioning specific people in your church who do humble tasks and are easily overlooked. Talk about how to express thanks to those servants of God.

Question 11. This issue makes for intriguing discussion, but take care to point out that the identification of spiritual gifts is a critical matter for serious Christians—not an opportunity for idle speculation. How can we discover our gifts? Many churches offer institute classes, exercises and inventories to help us identity those gifts that are ours. The best process, of course, is to rely on the Spirit himself to show us through our abilities, interests and inclinations just what our gifts are and how we are to use them to serve Christ's body.

Question 12. Verse 31 is really the lead-in to chapter 13, in which Paul explains that love is the greatest gift of all. Of course the original letter did not have chapters and verses. Paul views gifts as being greater and more desirable to the extent that they foster love and unity, strengthening the bonds between believers. To the extent that we use our energy to build the bond of fellowship between us that glorifies God, we are pursuing the greater gifts.

Study 3. Everyone's Invited. Philemon.

Purpose: To understand the principle of inclusiveness in Christian community, and to evaluate whether or not exclusivity is hindering your fellowship.

Question 1. Paul writes to Philemon, a Christian in Colossae, and to his household and the believers who meet in his home. Apparently Philemon's slave Onesimus stole from his master and ran away. Eventually he met Paul in Rome and became a Christian. Paul is sending Onesimus back (accompanied by Epaphras or Epaphroditus, who carries this letter and no doubt the letters of Philippians and Colossians). Paul urges Philemon to have mercy, to accept Onesimus as a Christian brother and very likely to free him. This is a radical request. Slavery was taken for granted in the Roman Empire. "The head of a household could legally execute his slaves, and they would all be executed if the head of the household was murdered" (Keener, *IVP Bible Background Commentary*, p. 642). Early Christian teaching began to change the master-slave relationship. Paul urged Christian masters to treat their slaves kindly (see Eph 6:9 and Col 4:1). In study two we saw that master and slave have equal access to Christ (1 Cor 2:13; see also Gal 3:28 and Col 3:11).

Question 2. Paul's tone is a positive one of affectionate praise and encouragement, combined with strong exhortation to act mercifully.

Question 4. Paul's praise of his readers is not only good diplomacy (since he is about to ask something of them); it also encourages and strengthens them for that task.

Question 6. The apostle knows he is dealing with a sensitive—and volatile—situation. To Paul's friends Onesimus must now seem a disposable person. Paul uses the slave's name to subtly make the point that in God's scheme, everyone is indispensable. Another pun on the Greek for Onesimus's name is found in verse 20 ("benefit").

Question 7. Paul has become Onesimus's spiritual father (v. 10), which can only mean that under Paul's influence Onesimus put faith in Christ, or at least began to mature in Christ. This fugitive thief is now fit to help the apostle Paul in his work (v. 12). Clearly Onesimus has repented of his wrongdoing and has become trustworthy.

Question 8. The social gap between Onesimus and Philemon is enormous. Besides that, the slave had committed crimes against the very household where the church meets (v. 2). If it is improbable that Onesimus will fit into this group of Christians, it is equally improbable that they will accept him. Onesimus is not the only one who needs to change. Philemon and his household must also rethink their values and their social attitudes.

Question 9. Paul makes a masterful appeal. He gives credibility to Onesimus as several times he affirms his affection for the slave. He confidently says that he knows he can count on Philemon to do the right thing of his own accord, with no coercion. He asks Philemon to treat Onesimus as he would treat Paul himself. He promises to pay back any loss, while he gently reminds Philemon that he himself is deeply indebted to Paul. He expresses hope that he will soon come to Philemon in person.

Question 10. "Acceptance" does not equal "membership." People may be on the membership list but in more subtle ways are not accepted.

Question 11. Luther has captured the many parallels here between Paul's work and Christ's. Onesimus would have legally faced a death penalty, for example. Paul intercedes and offers to pay the slave's debt. And now Onesimus can be "better than a slave, . . . a dear brother" (v. 16). This is just what Christ has done for us. Notice also the end of verse 19: "not to mention that you owe me your very self." Indeed, as sinners who had earned death before Christ interceded and paid our debt, we owe our very selves to Christ. Like Paul, we are to imitate him in being reconcilers.

Study 4. We Gather Together. Psalm 100.

Purpose: To identify the attributes of true community worship.

Question 1. In Psalm 100 one worshiper urges others—any who hear or read these words—to worship with him. It is not one individual saying "I worship alone." It mentions "all the earth" (v. 1) and "us" and "we" (v. 3). Even "all generations" (v. 5) implies more than one person.

Question 3. Although the psalm writer addresses his fellow worshipers, his true focus is the Lord who is to be worshiped.

Question 4. The psalm is sprinkled with imperative verbs: *shout, worship, come, know, enter, give thanks, praise*. These are all actions directed toward the Lord. They are not self-directed, such as *feel* or *enjoy*. Feelings or enjoyment can be a byproduct of worship but should never be confused with worship.

Question 5. Traditionally, churches and their sanctuaries have been designed to inspire worship and direct our minds and hearts to the presence of God. Of course we can worship anywhere. In Psalm 8, for example, the writer is inspired by God's natural creation. However, when believers gather for worship, they must necessarily come together in one place. Through the centuries believers have found or made such special places to praise God together.

Question 6. We thank and praise the Lord because the things stated about him in verse 5 are true. We are not told to enter his courts because we feel good, but because God is good. We are commanded to worship and be thankful, whether we feel it or not. It has been observed that we can act our way into feeling more easily than we can feel our way into acting.

Question 7. Thankfulness shows our respect and love for God. To take such gifts as physical life, forgiveness and eternal life in a spirit of ingratitude would be deeply disrespectful to the Giver. Our gratitude also shows our dependence on God. When we thank him, we acknowledge that he is the giver and we are receivers. We admit that we would have nothing and be nothing without him. Praise is our applause for how great God is. We can praise him for his many attributes, such as his mercy, love, justice and care. We can also praise him simply because he is who he is, the one God, our Creator.

Question 8. Just as we draw encouragement from others in any other activity, we can encourage and be encouraged by others in worship. Singing together is perhaps the most obvious example, but we also pray together, teach one another and learn together. Simply seeing other Christians and knowing we are not alone lifts our spirits to praise God.
Questions 9. Group members who have struggled with this issue may want to talk about their own experiences. Sometimes we avoid church because we have been hurt by other believers. Or we may be looking for a particular kind of worship experience that no church in our area offers. We may have let other activities—or simple inertia—replace the habit of going to church. The encouragement of Psalm 100 is especially appropriate for those who have drifted away or deliberately walked away from group worship.
Questions 10-11. "The Psalms did not originate as literary works, but arose in worship; they were spoken or sung in various ways and on various occasions of worship and were transmitted orally before they acquired written form in small collections" (Claus Westerman, in *The Interpreter's Dictionary of the Bible,* ed. George Buttrick et al., supplementary volume [Nashville: Abingdon, 1962], p. 705). The psalms, which were used for temple worship and by the early church, often told stories of God's love and faithfulness. Especially note Psalms 105—107. These stories of how God faithfully provided for Israel must have been a great encouragement during the Babylonian captivity and as the Jews later returned to the ruined city of Jerusalem.
Questions 12-13. It is one thing to take stock of our opportunities for corporate worship; it's another step to take advantage of them; and it is a further step to join in them wholeheartedly with an open spirit toward the Lord and our fellow believers.

Study 5. Community Commissioned. Luke 10:1-20.
Purpose: To understand the principles of evangelism in the context of Christian community.
Question 1. Some Bible translations may say "seventy" rather than "seventy-two." This is because some ancient Greek manuscripts of the Gospel of Luke say "seventy" and others say "seventy-two." Luke is the only gospel writer who tells of this larger mission in addition to the mission of the twelve. It would be exciting to be chosen and sent out by Jesus (v. 1), to be promised that their needs would be met (vv. 5-7) and to have spiritual authority (vv. 9, 19). On the other hand, Jesus indicated that danger and rejection awaited them (vv. 3, 10-12).
Question 2. Compared with the mission of the seventy-two, our own work

for the Lord may seem insignificant. Encourage group members to see that Jesus also chooses us and sends us out with authority to confront evil, and he does promise to meet our needs; on the other hand, we will inevitably meet up with danger and rejection as we do the work he gives us.

Question 3. Think of times you have accomplished things in partnership with others that would have been more difficult, even impossible, alone.

Question 4. The mission is urgent! The disciples should travel light and avoid material encumbrances that could disrupt their connections with people and their dependence on God. Jesus did not mean that they should be antisocial (after all, people were their destination), but that they should not be sidetracked on their mission. "Greeting no one on the way indicates the urgency of their prophetic mission representing God and not themselves; . . . it was offensive to withhold greetings, and pious people tried to be the first to greet an approaching person" (Keener, *IVP Bible Background Commentary,* p. 216).

Question 5. The key is to avoid distraction, whether by material possessions or by other involvements and interruptions.

Questions 6-7. Jesus' statement stresses the line connecting the Father to the Son to the believers. There is no way the world can know and experience God apart from our introducing them to Jesus. Indeed, there is no way we can introduce them to Jesus without access to power from the Father. We have the assurance of God's power for this work, yet we are also humbled—as "lambs among wolves" (v. 3)—by our helplessness without him.

Question 9. Jesus' language is strong and clear: when Christians carry out their marching orders, the kingdoms of hell are shaken to the ground, Satan suffers defeat, and the demons flee. As we fulfill our natural mission, it's important to maintain a supernatural perspective. "When Jesus speaks of seeing Satan's fall from heaven he is not thinking of an event from the remote past. He is thinking of the effect of his ministry at the time. He had sent out seventy of his disciples to spread the announcement that the kingdom of God had drawn near, and now they had come back from their mission in great excitement. . . . Many of the rabbis held that, at the end of the age, God or the Messiah would overthrow Satan. The report of the seventy showed that Satan's overthrow had already taken place, and Jesus' vision of his fall from heaven confirmed this. . . . The downfall of Satan may be regarded as the decisive victory in the campaign; the campaign itself goes on" (Walter C. Kaiser Jr. et al., *Hard Sayings of the Bible* [Downers Grove, Ill.: InterVarsity Press, 1996], pp. 465-66).

Question 10. We may compare our "results" with those of other witnesses, think our methods are superior, congratulate ourselves that God is blessing our efforts, become jealous and guard our turf from others, even become possessive about the work and imagine it is ours rather than the Lord's.

Study 6. Servant's Entrance. Matthew 25:31-46.

Purpose: To understand the importance of service as an imperative for the Christian community.

Questions 1-2. This is unmistakably the final judgment of humanity by Christ himself when he returns (v. 31). He is the "Son of Man" (v. 31) and "King" (vv. 34, 40) who comes with angels and takes his seat on a throne. The term "Son of Man" is Jesus' most common way of referring to himself. The term emphasizes his humanity and also his authority, since it is strongly connected to the authoritative figure in Daniel 7:13-14.

Question 3. "Although sheep and goats grazed together, it is said that Palestinian shepherds normally separated sheep and goats at night because goats need to be warm at night while sheep prefer open air. Sheep were more valuable than goats, and characteristics like this may have influenced how these terms would be heard figuratively" (Keener, *IVP Bible Background Commentary,* p. 118).

At the final accounting for humankind, it's clear that there are "sheep" (those whom the shepherd recognizes and claims) and "goats" (those who are not part of the shepherd's flock and don't belong). "The Son of man . . . sits on his throne before the gathering of the nations and separates them from one another as a shepherd separates the sheep from the goats (cf. Ezek 34:17). The sheep on his right hand represent those who serve him in this life. The goats on his left are those who refuse to serve him. But their destinies are not directly determined by their works. Rather, their works are determined by their nature as sheep or goats" (D. H. Johnson, "Shepherd, Sheep," in *Dictionary of Jesus and the Gospels,* ed. Joel B. Green and Scot McKnight [Downers Grove, Ill.: InterVarsity Press, 1992], p. 753).

Question 5. Some people may be startled and even fearful that they are lost because they "haven't done enough." The last thing this passage should do is send someone on a quest to rack up enough good works to earn salvation. Question 8 will deal more with this issue.

Question 6. Jesus focused on active, urgent aid to the helpless. He put this service at the center of both his life and his teaching. Yet many Christians miss the blessing of selfless service. In verse 34 ("Come, you who are blessed") and in Matthew 5 (the Beatitudes), Jesus implies that those who are involved in righteous living are being blessed here and now.

Question 7. A righteous person does not serve out of guilt, or sense of duty, or to earn favor, but out of true love and concern. With no self-consciousness, this servant helps wherever possible and is genuinely surprised to be rewarded.

Question 8. Obviously, a teaching of salvation by works would be a contradiction of all other New Testament teachings on the subject. We must remember this passage is a kind of parable and not a systematic doctrinal teaching. Salvation is purely by grace. The point is that those who are God's true children become involved in his work and "by their fruit you will recognize them" (Mt 7:16). His children have been about his business, and those who stand before him with no record of involvement in his concerns give evidence that they are not part of his family.

Question 9. Jesus means that if we want to serve God, we must serve people. He came to earth to identify with the lowly, and he calls us to do the same. Though we treated the King as a prisoner, we must treat each prisoner or poor person as if he or she were the King. This is not a statement that Jesus is in some real sense the needy person.

A charming legend about St. Francis of Assisi derives from this passage. At one time he was a wealthy young man with many worldly goods but no inner peace. Riding his horse through the countryside one day, he saw a leper with bleeding sores. Instead of recoiling in horror, Francis was oddly moved and was surprised to find himself dismounting and embracing the suffering man. As he did so the leper suddenly became Jesus. It is often only in the midst of service itself that we come to see the face of Christ.

Study 7. And They'll Know We Are Christians. John 13:1-17, 34-35.

Purpose: To understand the depth of love that is required in Christian community.

Questions 2-3. "The couches would be arranged around tables containing the food, with the upper part of each person's body facing the food and their feet away from the table. Jesus would go to the outside of this circle to wash each person's feet. After travelers had come a long distance, the host was to provide water for their feet as a sign of hospitality, as exemplified by Abraham (Gen 18:4). Yet loosing sandals and personally washing someone's feet was considered servile, most commonly the work of a servant or of very submissive wives or children" (Keener, *IVP Bible Background Commentary,* pp. 296-97).

Question 4. Peter was more eager to serve Jesus than to allow himself to be served by him. There is a kind of hidden pride in being unwilling to receive.

Just as we need to receive love and service, our brothers and sisters need to give it.

Question 5. On a deeper level, Peter needed to allow Jesus to "wash" him spiritually. Though Christ has cleansed our sin, we must accept his gift and continue to accept his daily cleansing.

Question 7. Verse 15 sums it up: if Jesus is willing to lower himself to a servant role for his disciples, we cannot presume to take a higher place or a superior role.

Question 8. We are to love each other as Christ loves us. This raises a question: If we do not love our brothers and sisters in Christ, do we really understand and appreciate the love of Christ for us? Perhaps we fail to love each other because we take Jesus' love too casually.

Questions 9-10. Our way of practicing community should startle the world, as it did in the days of the early church (vv. 31-32; Acts 3:42-47). The implication of this verse is that the world doesn't know how to love or else Christians would never stand out as they do. At the same time, the world expects us to love each other in a significant way, and they certainly notice when our love is no different from theirs.

Now or later. Your study group may wish to consider having a literal footwashing service.

Study 8. True Confessions. Nehemiah 9:1-5; James 5:13-20.

Purpose: To understand how God's community confesses sin to him and to each other.

Question 1. The mood is solemn but not despairing. In the people's repentance there is an underlying note of joy and hope. They are sorry for their own sins and for the sins of their ancestors (which brought about the conquest of Jerusalem a generation earlier). They are attentive to God's Word and they praise him.

Question 2. Fasting, wearing sackcloth and putting dust on the head were all signs of mourning and contrition before God. Sackcloth was "a garment of goat's hair or camel's hair, often worn as a symbol of mourning and by some prophets and captives" (W. L. Reed, in *Interpreter's Dictionary of the Bible*, 4:147). Recall that in study five, Jesus referred to "sitting in sackcloth and ashes" as a sign of repentance (Lk 10:13). Separating from foreigners was significant because Israel had often been led into idol worship by intermarriage with foreigners who did not believe in the true God. The people's outward preparation demonstrates their inward seriousness about repentance.

Question 5. God's Word always sets matters in their proper perspective as we begin to worship, pray or confess. It also allows God to speak a fresh word to us. In the order of this passage, the people first confess the sins they have in mind, then read the Word, then confess again (possibly the sins brought to their attention through hearing the Word), then worship—the natural response to God's activity and mercy in our lives.

Question 6. Church leaders should set an example in righteous living, but they should not pretend to be more righteous than they are. When leaders admit they are also sinners in need of God's mercy in Christ, they encourage the rest of the church to be honest about sin and come to Christ for forgiveness. Church leaders need not confess every sin before the whole congregation—in fact this would be inappropriate—but they should always present themselves as people who need God's grace as much as anyone else in the church.

Question 7. Verses 13 and 14 establish a pattern of individual action (if in trouble, pray; if happy, sing). But with the serious matter of illness, James advises us to call the leaders of the church to pray.

Question 8. There is power in community prayer that simply cannot be found in our individual supplications before God. Corporate prayer encourages us to confess sin and be reconciled to God and to each other. William Barclay wrote, "In sin there are two barriers to be removed—the barrier it sets up between us and God, and the barrier it sets up between us and our fellowmen. If both these barriers are to be removed, both kinds of confession must be made" (*The Letters of James and Peter* [Philadelphia: Westminster Press, 1976]). Whichever type of confession we find easier or more difficult, we must always keep in mind the importance of both "vertical" confession (to God) and "horizontal" confession (to one another).

Question 9. These events are recorded 1 Kings 17 and 18. Note that "Elijah was a man just like us," which relates to question 6.

Question 10. The sin of a Christian is not simply a private matter between that person and God. Sin affects the entire Christian community. Even if the sin itself remains hidden, it damages the sinner's spiritual influence and affects his or her relationships. No matter how carefully we hide our sin, other believers often sense that something is not right.

Study 9. Confrontation and Restoration. Matthew 18:15-35.

Purpose: To discover the principles of biblical discipline and forgiveness when sin enters the community.

General note. Do not allow this study to be an occasion to gossip or unnecessarily rehash old church business. Do encourage people to bring to surface their own sin or old conflicts with others that they may be harboring. Allow people to share in generalities or specifics as appropriate to the situation. Encourage one another to take practical steps toward reconciliation and to pray for each other. Also, be aware that sometimes reconciliation is a long internal process for each person involved and cannot be resolved with one conversation.

Question 3. Jesus is speaking to one who has been wronged by another. The conflict is between these two only. Some misuse this passage to confront a third party ("I heard that you did such-and-such to my friend").

Questions 4-5. Most conflicts can be settled between two mature people, and this should always be the first course of action. The purpose of bringing along "one or two others" is not to increase ammunition or stack the deck in our favor, but to provide objectivity and a reliable witness for what is said. In verse 16 Jesus is actually quoting Deuteronomy 19:15. Also, if too many people get involved in a personal conflict, the community may begin to choose sides, and a permanent split may result. Jesus says to involve the entire church only as a last resort if all other efforts at reconciliation have failed.

"Pagans and tax gatherers alike—tax gatherers were seen as agents of a pagan government—were excluded from the religious life of the Jewish community" (Keener, *IVP Bible Background Commentary,* p. 94). We might conclude that a Christian who has done wrong should be excluded from the church. But Jesus was criticized for befriending such "outsiders" as Gentiles and tax collectors. Matthew, a tax collector, became a disciple. We should never cut off our love from the offender. At the same time, if we truly love each other, we will not stand by and let either blatant sin or interpersonal conflict continue.

Question 7. Christians are the body of Christ. We act as he would act, and our decisions are his—as long as we act in the Spirit's power. "Ten Jewish males was the minimum quorum to constitute a synagogue assembly, but it was frequently said that God's presence was with even two or three who met together to study his law. Jesus' presence is thus presented here as identical with God's (cf. also Mt 1:23; 28:20)" (Keener, *IVP Bible Background Commentary,* pp. 94-95).

Question 9. Just as the man in the story is forgiven a financial debt he could never repay, we are forgiven a sin debt beyond imagination.

Question 10. Every time we behave without mercy, we are as guilty as the debtor in the parable. We ourselves have been forgiven an impossible debt and have escaped the terrible spiritual imprisonment which we earned. The man in the story either quickly forgot his enormous good fortune or else he had no concept of how much he owed. His promise to "pay back everything" (v. 26) indicates his inadequate comprehension of his debt. We must understand the depth of our sin before we can fully experience forgiveness and repentance. F. F. Bruce wrote, "The point of the parable was that one who has been forgiven a great debt will respond with great love, whereas no great response will be made by one whose sense of having been forgiven is minimal. . . . Love and forgiveness set up a chain reaction: the more forgiveness, the more love; the more love, the more forgiveness" (*Hard Sayings of Jesus* [Downers Grove, Ill.: InterVarsity Press, 1983], p. 80).

Study 10. A Haven for Healing. Ezekiel 34:1-16.

Purpose: To learn the healing responsibilities of the Christian community to its people and to commit ourselves to better nurture those who need us.

Background note. In study eight we read about the confession of the Israelites after their return to Jerusalem from exile in Babylon. Today's Scripture takes us further back in history, into that exile. Ezekiel was prophet to his people in captivity. He reminded them of the sins that had brought them down and of the righteousness which God requires. Coming from a priestly family himself, he directed strong words to Israel's leadership.

Question 1. They were lost and wandering (vv. 1-8), but God himself would rescue them (vv. 9-16). Note that *Israel* at this point does not mean "the land of Israel." The Israelites of the book of Ezekiel lived as defeated captives in Babylon (now generally Iraq), many miles from their home. The younger ones had been born in exile and had never even seen "home."

Question 2. Strengthening the weak, healing the sick, binding up the injured, bringing back the strays and searching for the lost are important ways the church cares for people. You might spend time discussing how the church does each of these. Note that the last two are directed outside the flock.

Question 3. The people were neglected (v. 3). Some were weak, sick and injured (v. 4). They had been ruled harshly (v. 4). They were scattered and lost (vv. 4-6). Without a shepherd, they were vulnerable to attack (v. 7).

Question 5. God himself said he would take responsibility for the scattered and lost sheep. He would also hold the false shepherds accountable. His words through Ezekiel give us reassurance that we are not at the mercy of flawed church leaders. While we should honor the leaders God gives us to guide our fellowship, our spiritual life is ultimately in the hands of the Lord, not any human being.

Question 6. God takes the initiative on behalf of his people. He does not wait for human help or for ideal circumstances. He cares enough to act.

Question 7. As disturbing as this passage can be, it's good to see the hope that emerges. God is justly upset at our lack of nurturing our people and seeking the lost, and he warns that the privilege of doing his work will be taken from those who have, in fact, abandoned the work. But we are all given peace in knowing that when people fail God's purposes, he finds other people and other ways to fulfill his purposes. God's love, patience and desire to reach us are boundless. We're comforted to learn that he will never abandon the needy, even when those he appointed to do so fail.

Questions 8-9. Remember from study two that no role in the church should be considered inferior. These questions pertain to any believer.

Question 10. This question is not meant to send anyone to scold a church leader. A better approach would be to offer help in the work.

Rob Suggs is a writer who devotes most of his work to the Christian market. He served for three years as a senior editor at Walk Through the Bible Ministries. He is also the author of the LifeBuilder Bible Study The Ten Commandments.